A Sequel to
*I am With You,*

# Abide in My Love,

Treasured words of
divine inspiration as given
to Fr John Woolley

First published by John Hunt Publishing Ltd, 2002
Paperback edition first published by O-Books, 2010
O Books is an imprint of John Hunt Publishing Ltd., The Bothy, Deershot Lodge,
Park Lane, Ropley, Hants, SO24 0BE, UK
office1@o-books.net
www.o-books.net

| Distribution in: | South Africa |
| | Stephan Phillips (pty) Ltd |
| UK and Europe | Email: orders@stephanphillips.com |
| Orca Book Services | Tel: 27 21 4489839 Telefax: 27 21 4479879 |
| orders@orcabookservices.co.uk | |
| Tel: 01202 665432 Fax: 01202 666219 | Text copyright John Woolley 2009 |
| Int. code (44) | |
| | Design: Stuart Davies |
| USA and Canada | |
| NBN | ISBN: 978 1 84694 276 1 |
| custserv@nbnbooks.com | |
| Tel: 1 800 462 6420 Fax: 1 800 338 4550 | All rights reserved. Except for brief |
| | quotations in critical articles or reviews, |
| Australia and New Zealand | no part of this book may be reproduced |
| Brumby Books | in any manner without prior written |
| sales@brumbybooks.com.au | permission from the publishers. |
| Tel: 61 3 9761 5535 Fax: 61 3 9761 7095 | |
| | The rights of John Woolley as author have |
| Far East (offices in Singapore, Thailand, | been asserted in accordance with the |
| Hong Kong, Taiwan) | Copyright, Designs and Patents Act 1988. |
| Pansing Distribution Pte Ltd | |
| kemal@pansing.com | A CIP catalogue record for this book is |
| Tel: 65 6319 9939 Fax: 65 6462 5761 | available from the British Library. |

Printed by CPI Group (UK) Ltd, Croydon, CR0 4YY

O Books operates a distinctive and ethical publishing philosophy in all
areas of its business, from its global network of authors to production
and worldwide distribution.

A Sequel to
*I am With You,*

# Abide in My Love,

Treasured words of
divine inspiration as given
to Fr John Woolley

BOOKS

Winchester, UK
Washington, USA

# Contents

# Introduction

*I Am With You* has already become established as a much-loved devotional book, in constant use by so many people throughout the world.

Further inspiring words from our Lord, received in times of prayer by Fr John Woolley, are contained in this new volume, *Abide In My Love*.

The life-changing and peace-giving words of the risen Lord Jesus, through His Holy Spirit, are certain to be experienced in this latest companion to *I Am With You*.

This little book offers unique help for the Christian's road and will prove indispensable for times of prayer and Bible study.

# 1

## Love's Brightness

**M**y love, though often only dimly realised, will always grow in the hearts of those who, at all costs, *abide* in it.

My love is the only true source of *lasting* light for the journey through this world.

My purpose through the ages has always been the awakening of a sense of My love in the hearts of My children.

Yes, there are forces dedicated to opposing this purpose, but it will not be denied.

My child, where My love is not realised there is darkness, and the outcome is disillusion.

**The light of the knowledge of the glory of God in the face of Christ Jesus.**

(2 Corinthians 4.6)

My child, My universe is constructed as it is, so that in all its apparent imperfections and contradictions, My love may be seen the more sharply, once it has been realised.

My love has to be *in contrast* to all the manifestations of a fallen world in order that it may have power in the lives of My children.

**The light shines in the darkness.**

(John 1.5)

3

It may be hard for the human race to understand, but My love gains power and poignancy as it is filtered through the pain and the apparent inscrutability of the created universe.

**Love is made complete among us.**

(1 John 4.17)

**M**y child, there are many false roads to knowledge of the Godhead. All of them prove bitterly disappointing.

The world's need is *only* met in Me – its *light*.

I came to earth not merely to 'reveal' the Father, but to *demonstrate* His love for all time.

Let it content you that, in Me, you are truly *enfolded* by the love of My Father.

### The only-begotten of the Father, full of grace and truth.

(John 1.14)

The *uniqueness* of My love is increasingly realised as you rely upon it! It begins to go beyond intellectual grasp and becomes your life's motivation.

You are able *both* to rise to effort and achievement and to be utterly rested in spirit by the same love.

As you feel more and more 'at home' in My love, you will reach the state of desiring nothing else ... which is the ultimate state planned for My chosen ones.

**I count everything as loss compared with the all-surpassing knowledge of Jesus Christ My Lord.**

(Philippians 3.8)

**I**f you are able to see *beyond* that which has been marred by the original rebellion against Myself, you indeed discover that all creation is love's expression.

My child, love is still triumphant in creation and you can *know* that, as you yield to that love, you are a part of that triumph.

### All things were created by Him and for Him.

(Colossians 1.16)

Love, as seen supremely upon the Cross, now ceased to be abstract, and apart from the struggles of mankind.

Such love now became a *power* in human hearts ...

**By His wounds we are healed.**

(Isaiah 53.5)

$\mathcal{A}$t the Cross, the essential *darkness* of a world from which I am so often excluded, could no longer be denied.

All the sense of life's futility, and all the heartbreak that can be the human experience, was seen there.

There, too, could be seen the bewilderment and the unfulfilled longings of mankind.

As it is contemplated, the Cross permits no lie about the *reality* of life on earth.

**In the world you will have tribulation.**

(John 16.33)

In spite of the agony there, the Cross becomes the place of hope ... even *before* My victory over death.

**It is accomplished.**

(John 19.30)

**I**f the Cross is deeply contemplated, it is saying that love is supreme, and that the darkness and the apparent unfairness of life can be endured.

In the Cross, love is able to speak ... speak to any human situation, whether of loss, of persecution, of disillusion.

### He laid down His life for us.

(1 John 3.16)

**A**lthough the Cross may be seen as a place of shame, the light of My love burned brightly for all who, in the succeeding years, would receive Me.

The Cross is saying that the pain of life cannot be avoided, but it is also saying that such pain can be transformed when the divine love is given an entrance. As pain is shot through by My love, heights of endurance and a patience undreamed of can be reached.

**Made His light to shine in our hearts.**

(2 Corinthians 4.6)

To the seeking heart there is the privilege of coming to an early realisation of the divine love ... present from the very beginning of existence, and giving existence its true meaning.

My child, I can already see the day of your complete release from worldly suffering! Share this vision with Me and let it help you to endure.

**God will wipe away every tear.**

(Revelation 7.17)

**B**ecause My love is the one reality, the one *permanency* of existence, the only true wisdom (not realised by so many), is to cultivate a knowledge of that love.

This is not easy in the setting of your world, with its deceptions and its discouragements, but if you simply show Me your *desire* to know My love, that is what I look for in order to reveal that love, increasingly, to you.

Is that desire there? If this is so, be assured that, knowing your heart, I am at work, *even now*, to grant you that priceless knowledge.

**Turn to Me with all your heart.**

(Joel 2.12)

14

**M**y child, can you see that the coming to your world at Bethlehem and the Cross of Calvary are *one whole*?

### He made Himself nothing.

(Philippians 2.5)

It is hard for mankind to realise that the love with which I created – on a scale which can only be dimly realised – was *focused* in the events of Bethlehem and Calvary.

These were places of the Divine *identification* with human suffering, which became a *lasting* identification.

**He took upon Himself our griefs.**

(Isaiah 53.4)

$T$he great power of My love upon the Cross produces the *miracle* of love in the previously loveless.

Love always awakens love – though a love that is still imperfect at the human level.

The divine love is able to provide a true and worthy *objective*, to which the barren heart can, at last, turn.

**We love because He first loved us.**

(1 John 4.19)

**M**y love, once realised, enables life to be held on to, where previously there may have been the desire to escape from life.

Realise that love is a *strength* in rescuing the faint-hearted.

My child always *see* My love as closer than every painful aspect. The *shield* of My love!

### Who can separate us from the love of Christ?

(Romans 8.35)

**M**y Incarnation transformed *knowledge* of your suffering into an eternal *sharing* of that suffering.

Such sharing will continue until you are released from all earth's bondages – because I have taken your humanity into the heavenly places.

**Made Himself poor ... that we might become rich.**

(2 Corinthians 8.9)

**W**here the light of My love illuminates a situation of suffering or despair, it shines *more brightly* than in any other surrounding or circumstance.

Love's brightness is readily seen, not only when confronting darkness, but when it is exercised sacrificially.

**In Him there is no darkness at all.**

(1 John 1.5)

**M**y child, the love behind the creation in which you are set is a place of *welcome* – shining around the hardest road, and enabling you to see that, in the end, all *must* be well.

Remember to rest, as a child, in that love:

> *whatever* the events …

> *whatever* the problems …

**His goodness and mercy will follow me all my life.**

(Psalm 23.6)

Almost always, the love I receive from My children is rooted in circumstances, far from perfect, often almost unbearable.

In this way, there is a faint reflection of the self-giving love from the Godhead – which is always a suffering Godhead, intensely conscious of human pain, and experiencing it.

### A man of sorrows.

(Isaiah 53.3)

It is vital that you do not listen to evil's lies, but always believe in your *worth* as My precious child.

No 'achievement' or 'lack of achievement' can in any way affect *My* love directed towards you as you are.

I require no intense effort – *only* the trust of a child who is greatly loved.

If you could but see how privileged you are as My especially chosen ...

**Bring the best robe and
put it on him.**

(Luke 15.22)

My child, remember that all disturbance of spirit is evil-caused. Meet it by an even greater *surrender* to the influence of My love.

Turn *immediately* from these intrusions of evil and let My love be victorious – restoring peace.

Keep your gaze upon My light.

Do not look away and falter.

Keep the word of *trust* upon your lips.

Never waver in your belief in My power to drive out evil and to heal the wounds caused by its inroads.

**Be strong in the Lord
and in His mighty power.**

(Ephesians 6.10)

**W**hen fear is strong ...

Let there be an earnest looking to My love.

If the sense of My love is strong, your mind cannot *simultaneously* hold a strong sense of fear.

Therefore, let My love's protecting arms lift you above the fear which darkens your mind.

Still looking to My love, express your thanks for victory over fear, and you will see that victory realised.

**Perfect love casts out fear.**

(1 John 4.18)

The reflections of My love in a human life may be seen as weakness. This is an illusion, because in that life there is a conquering power.

Many things conspire to hide the presence of My love upon earth, but it is the one supreme *fact* of existence, and eventually its light will be seen by all.

### My strength is made perfect in weakness.

(2 Corinthians 12.9)

I am never more truly at work than at a time of your being laid aside, through illness or weakness, which you have offered to Me.

**God chose the lowly things,
and the things that are not ...**

(1 Corinthians 1.28)

**M**y child, realise that waiting upon Me always ensures the *real* progress of your life.

### Only one thing is vital.

(Luke 10.42)

As you follow Me closely, the victories you win are largely unconscious!

**His power at work within us.**

(Ephesians 3.20)

Although some of My children may seem to be completely unable to respond to My love, and others may appear deliberately to reject it, the dimension of eternity must be remembered.

Just as to the human mind there is a vastness about My creation, there is a corresponding vastness about the welcoming realm of My love, and the working-out of My desire that no human soul should be lost.

**I will search for the lost.**

(Ezekiel 34.16)

No human soul – even those greatly disadvantaged, seemingly *lost* by the imperfections of your fallen world – is completely closed to My love's influence.

In the very depths of a human soul, no matter what is seen on the surface, there is a stirring of that love, as My love *guards* that soul for eternity.

**Nothing can take My children from My hand.**

(John 10.28)

$Y$our *appreciation* of Myself ... this is the key to appreciating what is of true worth in your world.

I am reflected in so many things, but this reflection can be missed if there is not the basic devotion to Myself. In many things there is only a *partial* reflection due to the inroads and spoiling activity of forces opposed to Me.

The hard lesson to be learned is never to be dazzled by any manifestation of creation other than that of My person.

As you keep centred upon Me, I will always light up for you that which can be trusted, that which can be responded to, in the material world.

My light is to dispel for you both interior darkness and all that surrounds you, in which the Divine presence has been obscured.

## I am the Light of the World.

(John 8.12)

**N**o matter at what stage of life My love is discovered, its effects are the same.

The element of hope has now entered, and the duration of that hope is limitless, as limitless as is My eternity.

As love turned darkness to light in the victory of the Cross, so it begins its work in darkened lives.

### That they, too, may be truly sanctified.

(John 17.19)

When circumstances seem beyond your control, it is important to remember My control, so that you can relinquish yours!

**He will not let your foot slip.**

(Psalm 121.3)

The opportunity is *always* there for you to leave all behind and to rise to a completely new quality of living.

All that is needed for this new life to start is the initial surrender of *every* aspect and then trusting Me, from that point, to overcome *all* with you.

My child, as you simply allow yourself to be lost in My love, I will do the rest!

### Come, follow Me.

(Mark 1.17)

$\mathbf{A}$n *empowering* light …

A light to draw out your worship …

As you consciously rise into it, other factors lose their power against you.

To live in My light is essentially to experience My *upholding*, because in that light, *love's* power is conveyed …

Yes, in love's shelter, fear *must* recede.

### The Lord will be your everlasting light.

(Isaiah 60.19)

**T**ry to see every present 'adverse' factor in its reality … as *able to contribute* to My purposes for you, as you give it to Me.

### Able to do immeasurably more than we can ever ask or imagine.

(Ephesians 3.20)

My child, where else can you find a love which is unwavering, understanding and all-sufficient in meeting every need that arises?

The greater the entrance to My love (by feeding upon it, thanking Me for it), the smaller is the field for evil to enter and lure you into dangerous by-paths.

Your *choice* to remain in My love, amid the distractions and varied circumstances of each day, means that our wills are then *in harmony*.

**Obeying My commands,
you will be kept in My love.**

(John 15.10)

**L**ove for Me is the great avenue to freedom. The imprisoned self is able to look to Me, absorb My love, and finally to reach out beyond oneself.

**The glorious freedom of
the children of God.**

(Romans 8.21)

**M**y child, the narrow way is the *easiest* way ... it is the way of repeated victories because of My unfailing assistance.

Along the narrow way (keeping your gaze upon Me and wishing above all to do My will), you can be sure that I go before you. I go before you ...

to open doors;

to smooth your path;

to send you those who are needed as part of my provision for you;

to over-rule.

Using the refuge of My love, evil is always rendered powerless against you.

**My sheep follow Me.**

(John 10.27)

**Y**our frequent realisation of how precious is My company.

An essential part of our closeness is our *ministering to each other*.

Our love-relationship to become stronger and stronger.

My child, I wish to be more and more aware of how thankful *you* are at possessing Me!

### I have called you friends.

(John 15.15)

Unless there was darkness in the created universe, unless there was darkness in the human experience, love would not be tested, and would be incomplete.

Without the element of darkness overcome, love is a transient thing.

**How wide and long and high and deep is the love of Christ.**

(Ephesians 3.18)

**Y**ou see the inseparability of My love and *light*. This is why I long for My children to lift up their gaze from the toils of earth towards the unquenchable light of divine love.

I long for that light to infiltrate every human experience.

Every turning to the light sets free the soul to enjoy the *influence* of My love.

### Walk in the light.

(John 12.35)

**T**he beauty seen in creation's higher aspects (in the natural world, or in human nature) is simply an imperfect reflection of the divine love.

See the beauty of *human* love (as it exists in children created in My image), as a light to reveal the truth of existence.

When true human love is seen in its radiance, it has taken on something of the divine creative love in its over-riding beauty and its permanence.

**The righteous will shine like the sun.**

(Matthew 13.43)

**H**uman love, rooted in darkness or pain – (love for Me, love for one's fellow human beings) is part of the great mystery of creation.

Such human love is then copying the divine love in being inextinguishable amid the forces of chaos, suffering and evil.

**Love always perseveres.**

(1 Corinthians 13.7)

**M**y child, we enter *together* the places where darkness apparently reigns.

The Creator, here, is essentially *Companion*. What would have been unbearable, has in it, now, the seeds of triumph.

**I will fear no evil for you are with me.**

(Psalm 23.4)

The look to My love and *all* is accomplished!

**Love never fails.**

(1 Corinthians 13.8)

$\mathbf{M}$y child, as acquaintance with Me grows, you realise the emptiness of life without Me.

The *acuteness* of how the emptiness is felt is only experienced by those who have loved and trusted Me when, for some reason, faith is temporarily lost.

The desperation to recover the sense of My presence when doubt occurs is merely a sign of the bond between us … a desperation which will always be met by faith's restoration because of My love for you.

**The incomparable riches of His grace.**

(Ephesians 2.7)

**M**y child, you are indeed wrapped around by My love and, more than all present details, *you* are My concern.

*Allow* Me to cherish you; *allow* Me to heal you.

Do not work against My healing by your striving or by *inviting* strain.

Everything shot through by My love. That is the way of true healing.

**I am the Lord who heals you.**

(Exodus 15.26)

**Y**es, My child – *close to Me* … your only safeguard. You are safe there from dangers of *all* kinds, including the spiritual. There, you are under a constant influence for good. There, you can simply surrender *all* care. Absolutely nothing is outside My control.

### He is our peace.

(Ephesians 2.14)

**H**ave you firmly taken My hand as the child who expects the *best possible* solution from what is given trustingly into My faithful love?

**The Lord will save,
and will rejoice over you.**

(Zephaniah 3.17)

$\mathcal{A}$ prayer (often repeated) asking for there to be *only* what is of Me.

This signifies your surrender to *My* influences around you and to *My* ways of using you and your surrender to the thoughts inspired by Me, rather than the distracting or harmful thoughts which the world can so subtly introduce.

Signifying reliance upon Me to make you aware of any intrusion which would be harmful as to where it might lead you and signifying that you will keep the light of My love at the centre, (feeling your *safety*).

Signifying your readiness to welcome whatever I send (so often unexpected and unplanned) and your readiness for Me to bring about what is in your best interests and in the interests of My children whose lives may touch yours.

**We are the clay; You are the potter.**

(Isaiah 64.8)

**M**y child, see in My followers through the ages ...

the *accentuation* of joy;

the *understanding* of sorrow.

Experiences of both darkness and light are heightened for you, as My follower, because they are increasingly experienced with My understanding.

### You will know the truth.

(John 8.32)

The shadow of the Cross is cast over all your struggles, as a sign both of My identification with them, and of My *victory* in them.

**I lay down My life for the sheep.**

(John 10.15)

**M**y child, are you remembering to see the dark thoughts, which enter your mind, as *intruders* rather than despairing of them as part of you?

Bring My *love* against them immediately so that you do not *dwell* upon these incursions of evil, nor feel led to act upon them. Thank Me for the *victory of My love* as you see it enveloping and excluding the intruder.

Every victory, (however small it may seem) deepens our effectiveness as a partnership.

**Put on the whole armour of God.**

(Ephesians 6.11)

55

The effect of My love in a person's life is essentially that of *uplifting* …

… an awakening of areas which may have long been denied expression.

The entrance of My love is the only factor which can ensure a life becoming what it was meant to be.

The more you feed upon My love, the more those around you will recognise that you are being *upheld*.

**He restores my soul.**

(Psalm 23.3)

The divine light – that of My love – *cannot* deceive.

Keeping within that light, the many pitfalls of life are avoided.

So much needless apprehension is due to *faulty perception* of circumstances, due to evil's lies.

**Christ will give you light.**

(Ephesians 5.14)

**M**y love is not to be seen as a *contra-diction* in the presence of human suffering.

Rather, it must always be seen as a strengthening, and as giving hope – however faltering, at times, that hope may be.

My love's *light* is one of both protection and healing.

### It is I; do not be afraid.

(Mark 6.50)

**E**ven in the darkest places, if there is merely the faintest awareness of My love, it is a *priceless* awareness.

'Priceless' is the true description not only of the gifts that I endow, but, above all, the gift, for *you*, of Myself.

Only the entrance of My love (to be coveted above all), can *fully* transform the world's darkness.

Nothing can surpass knowing Me or how very much I love you!

### A pearl of great value.

(Matthew 13.46)

Light, as found in the more desirable aspects of earth, is not light in its fullest and truest sense.

Only the divine light, entering earth's dark places, is seen to reflect Me in *completeness*.

### The Son is the radiance of God's glory.

(Hebrews 1.3)

# 2

# Love's Provision

As you contemplate the world's Saviour, see, in Him, the *Father* – inseparable from the Son.

See the Father's caressing arms as shield against the very worst aspects of earth's pain.

Because My love is both shield and source of power, we are able, *together*, to be invincible.

**Emanuel – God with us.**

(Matthew 1.23)

My child, value our friendship as the one which will *endure*.

It was to reveal Myself as *Friend* of mankind that I came ... willing to go to the very limits for My children.

Remember that same faithfulness is your inheritance. You can, therefore, feel completely at ease with your Maker and Sustainer who is also your Friend. Upon His understanding you can *always* draw.

**The Lord will delight in you.**

(Isaiah 62.4)

Under love's influence, every relationship is affected, every fret or anxiety simply melted.

Yielding to My love lifts you into the light of heaven ... the realm where I am always victorious, ensuring *your* victory.

**I can do all things through Christ who strengthens me.**

(Philippians 4.13)

**R**emember that nothing which is of the world should lessen your devotion towards Me.

It is *only* if I in-dwell whatever is of the worldly scene that your devotion is not diminished.

My child, *always* fly to Me when the lures of the world are strong and threaten our relationship. You will then once more prove that I give you what is the deepest satisfaction.

**Dear children,
keep yourselves from idols.**

(1 John 5.21)

The cycle of love ...

the divine love directed towards its children;

the return of love from those children, which gladdens My heart;

the continued out-pouring of My love.

**A spring of water
welling up to eternal life.**

(John 4.14)

**M**y child, in the *light* of My freedom, you are able simply to turn away from what is of darkness. The light will dispel the darkness for you whatever form it takes (whether the darkness is temporarily within you or in what surrounds you).

Always seeking My face, enabling your *direction* to be sure.

### If the Son sets you free, you truly are free.

(John 8.36)

In those hurt areas deep within your consciousness there may be *distortions* concerning My nature. That is why you must take every opportunity to dwell upon My *love* ...

### How much more valuable you are than birds!

(Luke 12.24)

**M**y child, can you see how I provide, and how I over-rule, as you tread My narrow way?

Following what your heart tells you to be right, you encounter endless instances of how I guide you and save you.

Contemplate how I have never failed you in life's situations thus far, and this will help you not to strive.

### I am the Way.

(John 14.6)

**M**y child, *allowing* My protection …
*allowing* My working.

My power on your behalf always means the
*least* effort of yours – especially effort involv-
ing reliance upon your purely human wisdom.

Yes, it is My *love's* power exerted upon you …

    healing,

    strengthening,

    guiding your steps,

    keeping evil influences at a distance.

My love is truly a *mantle* around you …
visualise it and be completely rested.


**Keep yourselves in the love of God.**

(Jude 21)

Intellectual knowledge will always be limited. That is why you need to throw yourself upon My love when mere thought can take you no further.

In this life, much will remain a mystery for you, but keep firmly in your mind the one-ness of My Father and Myself.

It is My Father *in Me* who comes to you, ministering to you. As you look to Me, see always the Father's love. This will be sufficient!

**Whoever has seen Me,
has seen the Father.**

(John 14.9)

My child, I am comforted that our relationship is a permanent one, and that you use *My* resources in a world largely indifferent to Me.

Centred upon Me, and with a trust which is *extravagant*, you will *never* find cause for regret.

**Lord, to whom else can we go?**

(John 6.68)

**A**s I have told you, your need is always *very* near to My heart.

As you express that need to Me, I cannot resist responding with My gift of *peace* to you.

Let My heart pour out its love to you, to refresh you ...

Let My love give you the courage which you need.

**If anyone is thirsty
let them come to Me.**

(John 7.37)

**A**lways trust Me to *act out of love* ...

**He will feed His flock
like a shepherd.**

(Isaiah 40.11)

The best possible foundation for facing what may lie ahead is the deepening of our friendship as the one which will embrace all others.

Realise that as you enjoy the comforting of My love, all the other aspects of your life are *simultaneously* under My good influence.

**Seek first for God's kingdom and all other things will be given to you.**

(Matthew 6.33)

**W**ounds of the spirit of long standing, which can affect the present, are *most surely* taken away by *every moment* that you spend consciously absorbing My love.

### He heals the broken-hearted.

(Psalm 147.3)

**W**hatever the circumstances, never be tempted by evil to abandon Me in favour of what is 'real'.

You will then *prove* that I have been with you, faithfully upholding you and blessing your circumstances.

**Let your true satisfaction
be in knowing Me.**

(Jeremiah 9.24)

**M**y word to you is that of *encouragement*. It could be no other!

Because every need of yours is My concern, you can quietly look for, and recognise, My *provision*.

Refusing anything other than to trust in My love and My greatness, you must *anticipate* that which I have in store for you.

### I am the Bread of Life.

(John 6.35)

**W**here you have trustingly allowed My working, you must not believe the lies of evil, that by doing so, you are allowing something to be neglected or are allowing events to go amiss. My faithfulness!

### Be anxious for nothing.

(Philippians 4.6)

**M**y child, you will not always find it easy to see the dark places as having any possible meaning, but you must hold very firmly to the thought of My *companionship*, and that My purposes *are* being served in anything that you have given (though with a heavy heart) to Me.

**Suffering produces perseverance.**

(Romans 5.3)

**D**id you feel very clearly, My peace in deciding upon a way forward, after surrendering to Me?

If this is so, *never* allow consequent doubts about that direction.

### He will watch over your life.

(Psalm 121.7)

**L**ife's secret – missed by so many – has been revealed to you. This is now your stability – both in inner conflicts, and in the fluctuations of earthly circumstances.

Never waver in seeing My love as life's meaning.

Feel My love's gentle pressure permeating all your being.

### The greatest of these is Love.

(1 Corinthians 13.13)

The only changes that *last* are those which My love produces.

Recognise My love's working in My provision, and in the changes which occur *without* your striving, having lifted up your situation to Me. *Respond* to such provision, and see it as pointing the way forward.

**Strengthened in the inner man.**

(Ephesians 3.16)

**A**s you prepare for the night hours, recall *both* My love's *inward* influence, and its *shielding* from the disturbances of evil.

As you rest in Me, consciously sink more and more into that love.

Never forfeit the renewal that is there for you as you return to the place of refuge after the varying fortunes of the day.

**He is my refuge and my fortress.**

(Psalm 91.2)

As you let yourself go, with no reservations, into My love, you find a *true* freedom in which I am able to save you from all evil's devices. Your growing freedom always rejoices My heart.

Do not delay in using Me as the *gateway* to freedom while there is time.

My child, the sense of My love to become more and more precious to you ... *There is no other way.*

**The Lord sets the prisoners free.**

(Psalm 146.7)

**M**y child, see us as a *permanent unity* – shielded from the dangers and deceptions of the world.

Feel the *security* of this unity – one in which the burdens of care are taken into My hands. Conscious of this unity, faltering steps are made sure ones.

**The name of the Lord
is a strong tower.**

(Proverbs 18.10)

**L**ove is effortless.

If My love fills more and more of your *thinking*, the result will be the carrying-out of My will automatically.

### My burden is light.

(Matthew 11.30)

**T**hanking and watching! ...

Your constant ...

*thanks* for My working;

*watching* for the results of My influence on your behalf.

### Why did you doubt?

(Matthew 14.31)

The greater the surrender, the greater My influence, and the more perfect the *outcome...*

### Take My yoke upon you.

(Matthew 11.29)

**T**reading the way with Me, the world's phenomena are seen in their true light and you realise increasingly that *only* My presence matters. Along that way, there is, all the time, healing of the spirit.

**Jesus Christ – the same yesterday, today and for ever.**

(Hebrews 13.8)

My child, for you there can be no more important role than ministering to Me, and comforting My heart.

**Jesus wept ...**

(John 11.35)

**M**y child, you know that your relationship with Me is of supreme importance. Let everything be in subservience to the relationship and *contribute towards it*.

Our relationship must always make the crucial difference. Your walk through a dark world then becomes one in which any weakness is *transformed* into an area of conquest.

**Given power from heaven.**

(Luke 24.49)

**W**hen you know the peace of My love you desire nothing else! You are *content* to await what I have in store for you.

### Rest in the Lord.

(Psalm 37.7)

**M**y child, yes, *all*-sufficient ...

Never be afraid to put this to the test.

## Is anything too hard for the Lord?

(Genesis 18.14)

$\mathbf{M}$y child, freedom is won by obedience.

Already you are assisted in treading the way of obedience. Each obedient step carries you further into the realm of freedom. Your steps now become increasingly *effortless*.

Where once there was only the will to please Me and great effort was often needed, you now become conscious of My lifting you.

Yes, the *using* of existing freedom means even greater freedom!

**Where the Spirit of the Lord is, there is freedom.**

(2 Corinthians 3.17)

The child ... one who *allows* Me to take responsibility.

**Because I created you,
I am able to carry you.**

(Isaiah 46.4)

**B**ecause of My working you are able to show *patience* ...

firstly, patience as circumstances are resolved under My hand;

secondly, patience with *yourself*!

### I shall not want.

(Psalm 23.1)

**M**y child, all the time I come to you ...

I come to you through so *many* things in My creation and into your heart by My Spirit.

The more you are *surrendered*, the more easily can My presence invade you, and the more easily can I minister to you.

**We will make our home in him.**

(John 14.23)

**M**y child, it is almost as if you are able to see yourself as *floating* upon that supporting love, as you let go earthly ties and restraints.

If only you could fully discern My love's working, you would be utterly at ease – content for Me to *support* you … content to endure, patiently.

The relationship between surrender and *provision* …

**The hairs of your head
are all counted.**

(Luke 12.7)

The only safe road to My eternity, (among the many roads claiming monopoly of the truth) is that which recognises Me, the world's Saviour, as the *absolute* expression of the Father.

*Any* environment in which I am expressly glorified is one in which the conditions exist for *drawing close* to Me.

### I and the Father are One.

(John 10.30)

**N**ever torture yourself concerning what appear to be the mere 'chances' of life – because this can lead to a form of superstition.

### I will trust and not be afraid.

(Psalm 56.4)

My child, let *Me* order what comes to you. Where this involves human agencies, ask that it should only be those of My special choosing.

Do not look to the world for what it is *unable* to give, but, rather, to what I (in My love) am supremely able to give.

Wherever possible, let those most profound heartaches be kept to share with Me.

Whenever you overcome *with Me alone*, a *gain* is always made.

**My grace is sufficient for you.**

(2 Corinthians 12.9)

**R**emember that there is nothing now existing that I cannot make right.

**With God all things are possible.**

(Mark 9.23)

**Y**es, refer *everything* that arises to Me initially. Allow My working and when any action is needed, let it be only *patient* action.

You are learning that My way is always easier and more direct than all others. Just let *Me* inspire your thinking ...

**Cast all your cares on the Lord.**

(Psalm 55.22)

**M**y child, remember that it is never the external 'details' of a situation that are crucial, but the attitudes of *individuals* in that situation, which are always influenced by your prayers.

Always seek first, My work, in the *hearts* of those involved.

### Pray continually.

(1 Thessalonians 5.17)

**E**vil would distort events to produce extreme agitation about things where no danger lies – things not worthy of your thought, and which only distract from Myself.

*Feel* My love undertaking for you in *every* aspect of evil's tempting, as you *allow* it to do so.

Remember that as you use the shelter of My love, evil is *made powerless*.

### The devil is a liar.

(John 8.44)

It is not a question of striving to 'feel' strong against temptations; rather, letting the sense of My love weaken those assaults.

It is the sense of my love which ...

enables you to know that all is made right again when you stumble;

disperses the guilt, the sense of failure, upon which evil can play.

**God is greater than our hearts.**

(1 John 3.20)

**M**y child, does your life fit trustingly into *My* working? Because your heart is Mine, I lead you very surely.

Allowing My working, you need only pursue what is clearly *yours* to pursue and, even then, it will require My blessing.

**Without Me,
you can do nothing.**

(John 15.5)

**V**ictory is never more sure in *any* adverse circumstance than when you have remembered to see evil as its underlying cause, and then to stand against such evil with Me.

Once you have learned to stand up to evil, in My strength, *no other* challenges of life can daunt you!

**Resist the devil,
and he will flee from you.**

(James 4.7)

**M**y child, if you keep your eyes upon the light, in spite of all distractions, you become aware of how all-encompassing is My love – a love in which you can rest *completely*.

Yes, it is above all a protective love, enabling you to walk with confidence in My forbidding whatever would be harmful.

Your feeling of security should always be accompanied by expressions of gratitude and trust. In this way, there is always a *mutual receiving*.

### His banner over me is love.

(Song of Songs 2.4)

The *carrying* of My love is a process of which you may not always be aware – until you see the results of My upholding. Therefore, My child, ensure *early* that to live in My love is your *primary* desire. I can then respond by proving to you that love's resources are *limitless*.

**The Father knows your need.**

(Matthew 6.8)

$O_{nly}$ My love ... its conquering influence ... its whole-making influence.

As you yield, constantly, to that love, it will always prove stronger than the *condemning* voice of evil.

Believing the best of Me always begins with the inner certainty of My love.

### Each day I will bless you.

(Psalm 145.2)

As you return to Me in both repentance and surrender and *side with Me* against whatever caused you to stray, the *consequences* of straying are made to serve a purpose beneficial to you, even if you do not perceive it.

**There is no condemnation for those who are in Christ Jesus.**

(Romans 8.1)

**M**y child, a consciousness of how *much* you have in Me!

Remember the rewards in *this* life of conquering in My strength ... the rewards of peace, and of an ever-deepening faith.

As you use My strength in dismissing evil's assaults, you can *know* that My strengthening remains for further conquests!

**Overcome evil with good.**

((Romans 12.21)

You have the *constant* enfolding of My love, as you trust that love in striving to survive within the sphere of this present existence … otherwise the journey would be impossible for you.

Always be grateful that My love brings you through the *hidden* dangers.

Ensure that My name of power is upon your lips in negotiating the hazards of a fallen world.

**The Lord is my strength and my shield.**

(Psalm 28.7)

So often you will turn to Me with a sense of desperation, or even of anger.

Although it will not always be easy, let your turning to Me be one of *confidence* and *thankfulness*, as you allow the thought of My love and My faithfulness.

The pressure of circumstances will then start to respond to My presence!

**God's unfailing love surrounds
the one who trusts in Him.**

(Psalm 32.10)

**N**othing can go seriously amiss (in spite of the world's misfortunes and its misunderstandings) if you have set out with the steady aim of pleasing Me, and if you constantly return to Me with the surrendered will.

I continue to weave everything into My pattern for your life in order that it may help, in some way, your eventual perfection.

**All things work together for the good of those who love God.**

(Romans 8.28)

If you can ignore feelings and circumstances and set out in spite of these, in the path of trust, I will always honour this by *relieving* you of obstacles and discouragement along the way.

Even when disappointments come, continue *courageously* along the way of trust, ready once again to experience My provision and My blessing.

**Before they call, I will answer.**

(Isaiah 65.24)

It is because you do not possess My knowledge that you simply have to trust, utterly, My sure working.

Often in the most unlikely situations I am faithful to give Myself to others through you.

My *influence* permeates your existence to convey what is able to serve My purposes.

### All power in heaven and earth belongs to Me.

(Matthew 11.27)

**H**ave you learned to see *every* circumstance as working for you – even the painful ones?

All because you are My *concern*! ...

**He is faithful in all that He does.**

(Psalm 33.4)

As you refuse to stray – in your thoughts, in casual words, in commitment to action – you will find, to your great joy, that you are being lifted by a power which is not your own.

Repeated thanks and expressions of trust will *maintain* that assisted walk. You may not always recognise it, but it is the walk leading to life. Every step, surrendered to Me, consolidates your inheritance.

**Blest are the pure in heart.**

(Matthew 5.8)

**L**asting harm can only be avoided by your consciousness of My company. If I am in your gaze, the journey with Me becomes instinctive.

'Carried' is no figure of speech … it is the *experience* of all who hide in Me.

### Your life is hidden in Christ.

(Colossians 3.3)

The journey taken with Me is the journey of the working-out of My purposes for your world!

You are then used in so many ways (*never* unimportant) in My plan for mankind.

Allying yourself with the creative power of the ages, you then simply submit to My gentle leading.

My child, rejoice in My using you as a *chosen* child with all the blessings which are yours upon the way.

**Created in Christ Jesus
for good works.**

(Ephesians 2.10)

Always the extravagant trust in Me.

Allow no diminution of My person from any source. Only those who do not really know Me have reserve about what I am able to do.

For My followers, it must be a case of 'all or nothing' because on this depends My loving intervention.

I require, always, the abandonment to My love's comforting presence and its simultaneous power to affect every situation for you.

My child, bring to mind, often, the vast design of creation, and then, within that, see your Creator's mindfulness of *your* need at every moment. As you do this, it will never permit of any doubt.

**Who do you say that I am?**

(Matthew 16.15)

$\mathbf{A}$lone with Me ... the greatest privilege.

Keeping the company which will one day be yours to the full.

Rejoice in this privilege – it is the only *true* source of lasting joy.

Frequent *recognition* ... as you simply relax in My love.

Always a light to turn to in the surrounding darkness.

*My* suffering love sheds its light upon *your* suffering, helping you to find peace in My sharing.

A light of victory, as the past is rendered harmless; a light of victory, as all present concerns have to fade in their clamour.

**In You, O Lord, I have taken refuge.**

(Psalm 71.1)

125

# 3

# Love's Journey

The dangers inherent in your world are many. There is the exercise of human wisdom, divorced from submission to that love.

Unless My love is *allowed* its influence there is always error. Unless My love is *allowed* its influence, the seeds of destruction are sown.

The forces opposed to Me are rendered powerless, not by show of strength, but by the victory of My *love*.

**By God's power we live.**

(2 Corinthians 13.4)

**M**any fail to see that the greatest good they can do is to give Me their attention …

My child, that attentiveness to My love automatically produces the obedient walk.

The transforming power is seen both in the child who maintains the gaze upon Me, and in the wider field of that child's relationships and circumstances.

**Lead me in a straight path.**

(Psalm 27.11)

The realisation that, *without* Me, your fallen world has a very limited amount to offer … only transient joys.

This realisation has to become the *experience* of those who desire to live in the full knowledge of My love.

**Set your mind on things above.**

(Colossians 3.2)

**S**ee the many facets of My love as it works in the human heart.

Love as patient as the creative process ...

Love as wise as the creative process ...

Love as sure as the creative process ...

Love as *light-producing* as the creative process ...

Always give time for My love to *exert* its influence upon you in *every* current situation, and, of course, in situations yet to be entered.

**I am making everything new.**

(Revelation 1.5)

ondering the Cross, and the road which I endured, will give you a sense of My sharing, and give you a courage which otherwise would not be there.

**Remain united with the vine.**

(John 15.4)

My child, resist evil's attempts to perpetuate, *through memory*, that which no longer exists in My sight.

Do not listen to its lies for one moment.

Bring My love against evil's attempts to revive the torture of guilt.

You know that where you have sought and received My forgiveness, nothing exists for you but My love – ensuring your peace, and still affecting all the events of your life.

**I will both forgive and forget.**

(Jeremiah 31.34)

Take care that your true self, your best self, is never *overlaid*.

Evil can ensnare you into filling your life with things not serving My purposes.

Surrender every passing affection, every passing interest, which prevents you from being the calm and purposeful person I desire – an influence for good in the world around you.

Do not *starve yourself* of My love. A life following after too many things starves not only itself, but others, of My love.

**I must be first in your affections.**

(Exodus 20.3)

There are so many occasions when I ask *nothing more* of you than to rest your spirit in My love.

This *ministers* to Me as much as all your practical activity on My behalf, and will always prove a source of blessing for you.

**Come to Me.**

(Matthew 11.28)

**I**f you cultivate a life that is peaceful and prayerful, evil is vanquished, increasingly, as I greatly use you.

Nothing will go amiss as you act with trust, and with restraint. Your obedience will then result in everything falling into place.

Hidden in Me, let there be

*only* trust …

*only* peace …

*only* joy …

*only* hope …

**In quietness and confidence will be your strength.**

(Isaiah 30.15)

**W**ish earnestly for your life to be more and more a copy of My own in ...

its love,

its serenity,

its purity,

its courage,

its patience.

My child, see everything not of love as unworthy of your concern ... it is of an inherently passing nature. Allow nothing but the *peace* of My love.

### Partakers of the divine nature.

(2 Peter 1.4)

**M**y child, the lesson is a hard one, and needing often to be repeated: *utter* surrender to My working.

You realise that circumstances will never be perfect, and that is why there must be that constant committal of those circumstances to My safe handling.

In response to the merest trusting *consent* on your part, the divine power, which works for you, becomes *your* power. You are then used in a natural way, responding to what I send.

### I will strengthen you.

(Judges 6.14)

The peace that you feel upon the narrow way is not an illusion; it becomes something that you take for granted – something that you do not have to plead for.

When peace is lost, come to Me for restoration, and for Me to bring to nothing the effects of what may have caused you to stray.

Do not seek to 'feel' peace immediately – simply be sure that you rejoin the narrow way, with everything *surrendered anew* to Me. Peace will be restored, as you go forward again in My companionship.

**Walk in the good way, and you
will find rest for your soul.**

(Jeremiah 6.16)

**R**emember that our unity is your defence against dangers which are not only seen, but which are unrealised!

Trust My help in recognising, *from the very outset*, when you are in danger of departing from the way of trust. See My love hurt by such deviation, and capitulate once more to that love.

Love's victorious march! Forces opposed to Me recognise when you are embraced by that love, and are compelled to retreat.

### Be sober, be vigilant.

(1 Peter 5.8)

**M**y child, nothing need surprise you as we travel together through the darkness of this world, because, with Me, you are ready for *anything*.

I always chart the *right* path of circumstances for you as you are centred upon My love.

Enjoying the *influence* of My love in preventing evil from leading you into what would be spiritually harmful.

### The armour of light.

(Romans 13.12)

**M**y child, walk uprightly, with confidence, and always with a very firm direction.

I will always alert you to *real* danger. You can then *allow* My help in rising above that which is not indwelt by Myself.

Your concern, constantly, about *everything* in life which is *of Me*.

**Do not be conformed
to the pattern of this world.**

(Romans 12.2)

Life is *drastically* changed when I am followed, and your walk becomes one not only of trust, but of utter simplicity, free of compromise.

My child, though beset with danger, that narrow way, negotiated with Me, proves to be the true way of safety because upon it, your *spiritual* progress is unimpaired.

Remember that the fixing of your gaze upon Me, very resolutely, means that so many subtle and distracting obstacles are unable to touch you.

The peace of heart which you experience upon My way is in no way dependent upon the fortunes of life.

**You will keep in perfect peace
him whose mind is steadfast.**

(Isaiah 26.3)

**T**ry to see yourself as apart from the darker manifestations of the old 'self'. Instead, be increasingly identified with your true self – that which hates wrongdoing.

Let Me shield that true self from the guilt and fear and recurring pain to the mind which indulgence of the former self inevitably bring.

**Transformed into His likeness.**

(2 Corinthians 3.18)

**M**y child, do not set impossibly high targets for yourself, as I carry you gently forward. I have made it clear to you that the *fact* of spiritual progress is more important than the *rate* of progress.

**Christ in you – the hope of glory.**

(Colossians 1.27)

**W**henever possible in complexities, 'follow your heart' if that heart has been given unreservedly to Me, and your will utterly surrendered.

### The wisdom which is from above.

(James 3.17)

**M**y child, is your aim that of building a relationship which depends on Me alone – in which *everything* carries My involvement?

All I look for is your *consent* to what I am then uniquely able to bring about.

**Ask – and it will be given you.**

(Matthew 7.7)

**T**he link between obedience and healing ...

Can you see that whenever you make the effort of obedience, strengthened by Me, it is a conquest of evil, with a *lessening* of its influence deep within you?

This always assists My healing of spirit, mind and body.

My child, *thank* Me for My healing influence, as you look to My light and *worship*!

**Risen with healing in His wings.**

(Malachi 4.2)

**M**y child, allow My love to be *dominant* throughout each day ... resolutely refusing all that is not of that love, and the peace which it gives.

The more you feed upon My love, the more *sure* will be the path which you tread.

The gaze towards My enfolding love should always be accompanied by a sense of gratitude for My sure working – whatever the circumstances.

The times which you share with Me are times when you truly enter *eternity*.

### The love of Christ
### which surpasses knowledge.

(Ephesians 3.18 and 19)

**R**emember that I only allow you to see areas of darkness in your nature, (an often painful recognition), in order to bring you into the realm of My light where, in you, My name can be glorified.

You are realising that those very deepest desires (those you cannot perfectly share with others) can *only* be met if you share life with Me.

**Inwardly we are renewed every day.**

(2 Corinthians 4.16)

150

$\mathcal{A}$ *balance* ...

Firstly, *accepting* circumstances that I permit after your submissive prayer.

Secondly, the exercising of your judgement, carefully, as I prompt you.

The thought of Me as your *refuge* will help you to be steady and clear in your judgements.

Decisions (using your free will) will then be *informed* decisions.

### Whoever follows truth will walk in the light.

(John 3.21)

It is so important to use what I have given you, both for personal victories, and for the benefit of others. No vocation can equal that of being led by Me in surrender, *knowing* that I will always, in some way, be using you.

Is the thought of a particular demand a daunting one? Lift it up into My love and *see* Me carrying you through.

My love will *always* minister to you in what is seemingly impossible in human terms. Let Me prove this to you.

**My God will meet all your needs,
according to His glorious riches
in Christ Jesus.**

(Philippians 4.19)

**W**hen there is human ill-will towards you (recognised or otherwise) be assured that harmful *effects* from it are prevented because of your trust in Me.

When you sense that you are being opposed, always resort first to prayer, rather than persuasion or anger.

Power is then released!

**Pray for those who persecute you.**

(Matthew 5.44)

**M**y child, I want you constantly to receive My love – feeding upon it without fretting for any other consolation.

Yes, My child, *receive* My love …

And give *only* My love!

**Come, all you who are thirsty.**

(Isaiah 55.1)

**M**y child, ensure *every* day that I am the paramount desire of your heart. If this is so, the sense of My love and companionship will always be with you.

Do not, then, doubt that I will shape *all* your life's events.

Remember that, as you surrender that which you sense is not for your highest good, I will always provide that which is of *lasting* worth.

Ensure that the 'I' (in all its forms), is removed from the centre of your existence, so that you increasingly lose yourself in all that *I* am.

**Blessed are those who hunger
and thirst after goodness.**

(Matthew 5.6)

**W**hen the way is clouded, it is more than ever the time for keeping strictly to the narrow path of My revealed will, *already* given to you. Concentrate upon observing what you *know*, standing upon the solid ground of Myself. As you follow the wisdom instructed by Myself (with no fear of men), deception is avoided.

**The road to destruction is broad.**

(Matthew 7.13)

You need never feel overwhelmed by the many precepts that you feel you must follow, if you ensure *consolidation* in areas where you have begun to be victorious.

Try never to retreat into ways of weakness, which you were beginning to leave.

If a lapse occurs, let it serve only to produce a *more complete* surrender to Me.

### So then ... stand firm.

(2 Thessalonians 2.15)

**R**emember that to be a true channel of My love, you must ensure that your motives are *purified*.

Through the life *wholly dedicated* to Me, I *always* reach out.

The stronger your consciousness of My love, the greater is the power at work through you.

Always find the deepest satisfaction if My purposes are *your* purposes.

### Who, then, is the faithful and wise servant?

(Matthew 24.45)

**M**y child, let nothing – no worldly concerns – interrupt My Spirit's healing flow.

Be rested …

Be courageous in facing what life produces …

And, of course, make *everything* the subject of prayer.

**Do not let your heart be troubled.**

(John 14.27)

The victorious walk always has My love in mind! Obstacles to My purposes for you are then made to fall away from your path.

As you keep close within My love, the walk becomes one in which you do not constantly need to consider whether or not you are pleasing Me. Instead, a *natural* obedience.

**This is to My Father's glory,
that you bear much fruit.**

(John 15.8)

**D**oes a proposed course of action conflict, in any way, with all that you know of Me? Is it one in which you cannot feel that I am comfortably 'in it' with you?

Never tolerate through *expediency* any action that you know, instinctively, is contrary to My will.

Always give time to establishing these things before committing yourself to the course of action, remembering that My love is hurt by what is wilful or hasty.

**I will counsel you
and watch over you.**

(Psalm 32.8)

**W**here My love's influence lives, evil cannot live.

All wrong *desires* are extinguished where My love is able, by its influence, to conquer.

Let Me fit you increasingly into *My* design ... an obedient vessel of love, trust and submission.

My child, the value of repeating your trust in Me in order to *wear down* evil's lies.

### If God is for us, who can be against us?

(Romans 8.31)

**R**emember that when you come to Me for a new start after failure, I mould circumstances in your favour *from that point*.

### Rich in mercy.

(Ephesians 2.4)

**M**y child, at all costs guard against anything which could cause you to lose the sense of My love. To be My chosen carries the *privilege* of becoming sure of My love in a precarious existence.

As I have told you, My love is the one unchanging aspect of your life into which everything else *must* fit.

### I have called you by name; you are Mine.

(Isaiah 43.1)

$\mathcal{T}$here will be times when you hastily make a promise that proves to have been misguided.

Remember that if, in absolute abandonment to My will, I subsequently show you a better way, you are not held to such a misguided promise and need not be in self-condemnation if it is not fulfilled.

**Let this mind be in you**
**which was in Christ Jesus.**

(Philippians 2.5)

**R**emember that *only I* know a person's true situation.

Therefore, resist the lies of evil, which make you see a person's circumstances superficially.

So often, an individual has hurt which is concealed. Do not covet that which is passing in what that person appears to possess.

Possessing Me, *you* have so much!

**Be content with what you have.**

(Hebrews 13.5)

**R**emember that evil works to *pre-occupy* you with anything which will take you away from the quality of life which I wish for you.

The intrusions of evil are, in so many ways *pathetic* intrusions; they emanate from a force which cannot ultimately stand against Me.

When evil attempts to haunt you through painful memories, very deliberately hand back the subject of the disturbance to Me and let My love dissolve it.

### Look to Me and be saved.

(Isaiah 45.22)

When you sense that you have been tempted to strive, return immediately to resting in My love until the time to act again, *with patience* is made clear.

Never let *fear* cause you to act against what I am making very clear to your heart.

**Let patience have its perfect work.**

(James 1.4)

**E**nvy of others' happiness or wellbeing can occur if one feels in any way 'deprived'.

But remember, my child, that such envy, (though it may seem 'natural') reflects the mind of evil which opposes Me.

Ask therefore, that you may have *My* mind, which rejoices in the good which comes to My children, and never in their misfortunes.

Let My love for you spill over into all your attitudes towards others; you are helped to do this by remembering, with gratitude, that My love towards you is *permanent*.

### You shall not covet.

(Exodus 20.17)

As you (with acceptance), watch day-to-day events taking place under My hand, do not be tempted to change a course of events out of fear, or because of any unworthy motive.

Yes, *yield* to everything which I allow – praying thankfully as you watch the way unfold. As you submit to My ordering, all will fall into harmony.

As an obedient child, you are My partner in helping to *make* the road ahead!

**The obedience which
comes from faith.**

(Romans 1.5)

Consciously to rest in surrender to My love is not 'passive', because it creates the right conditions for My unerring *activity*.

Let your walk with Me, now, *reflect* the truth that all is in My hands. Never fail to thank Me for this truth.

My child, be sure to *apply* My promises to your life …

**Do not worry about tomorrow.**

(Matthew 6.34)

My child, I have told you that it is a question of looking at the world through My eyes, seeing what is of *lasting* worth, and rejecting all else.

Always remembering the *passing* nature of the varied causes of fret encountered on your daily walk.

**What is unseen is eternal.**

(2 Corinthians 4.18)

**M**y child, again I tell you ... *all* is of My love.

As you yield to its influence, not one aspect of life is untouched by Me. Do not in any way restrict or weaken this.

Therefore, journeying in My love:

    not the slightest element of striving;

    not the slightest agitation of spirit;

    not the slightest apprehension.

Ensure that in every situation, we confront it *together* ...

**Able to keep you from falling.**

(Jude 24)

So much danger is avoided for a child who keeps a *constant longing* for what is of Me.

Repeatedly giving yourself unreservedly to Me you will feel a sense of hope *from that very moment* – even though daunting circumstances remain.

My child are you *literally* resting in My love, refusing to respond to circumstances which arouse anxiety?

Let Me support you unfailingly in those struggles which the world does not see!

**Being with you,
I desire nothing else on earth.**

(Psalm 73.25)

**M**y child, the *very* narrow way is only negotiated with the closest possible attention to Myself. You are able, as I have told you, to *steel yourself* to tread My path, refusing discouragement, knowing that all I have for you is coming about.

As you desire *only* what I will send, you will discern what is safe and which carries a blessing.

Expect evil's lures. Expect to be enticed into lowering your standards. I will never fail to lift you above such dangers, as you turn from them, deliberately.

My child, *refuse all over-elaboration*, which gives evil the soil in which to introduce confusion.

### Pruning ... that the branch may bear much fruit.

(John 15.2)

# 4

## Love's Destination

Let every day begin with the *acknow-ledgement* of My love. Let that love help you to put aside (even if only for moments) all the agonising prospects, the causes of heartache, which are presented to you.

In My love's light those darker aspects are better able to be faced. Continuing to look to My love, the darkness is diminished in its power, and it can then never completely over-whelm you.

**Do not fear, for I am with you.**

(Isaiah 41.10)

**R**emember to see not only *yourself* as enveloped by My love, but every *circumstance*.

In that love, completely trusting Me, your only feeling must be that of peace.

Use every occasion of lapsing into anxiety as a *reminder* ... In your mind should be the countless times that I have brought you through!

### The shield of faith.

(Ephesians 6.16)

**W**hen a time of darkness is pierced by a feeling of hope – even for a few moments – this is always a sign of the beginning of healing at a deep level.

My promise to make all things new applies at *any* time to *any* circumstances.

In My sight, the past is as if it had never been.

**Those who sow in tears
will reap with songs of joy.**

(Psalm 126.5)

**M**y child, I know that you will be constantly alert to what may temporarily divide us …

There are always factors to worsen a situation, or to send you dangerously astray.

If you keep close to Me, I will always make you aware of your progress being obstructed and you can trust Me to check you.

Waste no time in then returning to the thought of our *unity* within My love.

**I am the vine; you are the branches.**

(John 15.5)

**T**ry to see My love as the *rock* of your life. By comparison with My love's permanence, all that gives you pain is, in *My* sight, in the nature of 'what will pass'.

All your pain will eventually yield to My presence as you repeatedly *cast yourself* upon the rock of My love, knowing that My love is all that will remain for the soul which trusts Me.

### An inheritance incorruptible.

(1 Peter 1.4)

If you have deliberately taken My hand, I lead you, very gently, *without* your seeing the full extent of what lies ahead.

What is outside My purposes for you is then kept out.

The gaze into My love for strength, for understanding, for wise prompting in perplexities ...

The peace of surrender to My love!

**I will give you rest.**

(Exodus 33.14)

**T**he direction of love is always an upwards one, because you are then avoiding the diversions which would spoil your progress.

It is love's *light* which draws you inexorably upwards.

A journey of *My* promptings and of *My* opportunities.

**He Leads me in paths
of righteousness.**

(Psalm 23.3)

**M**y child, sense that it is Myself walking though the world in you ...

   guiding your footsteps,

   strengthening,

   enlightening,

   blessing others.

Let Me draw you along the heavenward walk ... frequently looking towards your goal.

Realise increasingly that you are sheltered from a hostile world as I allow *only* to cross your way that which is for your good.

### The Lord will keep you
### from all harm.

(Psalm 121.7)

My child, always see the *unimportance* of what is tainted by the world so that you can give yourself more completely to what is of Myself.

See the *unimportance* of every present circumstance, compared with your *destiny*.

**To see My glory.**

(John 17.24)

$\mathfrak{A}$s your duty, constantly thank Me that *all* is in My hands.

My child, *nothing* is allowed (no seeming 'chances'), which cannot further My eternal plan for you.

Reflect on the fact that you will eventually see how present events have facilitated My will and be filled with gratitude.

**I will never forget you.**

(Isaiah 49.15)

Yes, life is essentially a learning experience ... gathering knowledge of Myself, and gaining insight into the supernatural conflict which is the background to life upon your earth.

*Only* if you consciously allow Me to accompany you, does life become a true learning experience. Only then does life become a thing of *progress* towards mankind's destiny.

## Learn of Me.

(Matthew 11.29)

The love of which I have spoken can *only* forgive when there is a turning to Me. My work in eternity is to create a place where a human soul can come to desire Me, and leave behind all rebellion of spirit.

My child, in your present existence, such wooing of the soul may not be apparent, but in the realm of My eternity there is a *continuance* of the revelation of My love glimpsed upon earth.

### I will receive you.

(John 14.3)

**M**y great gift of *hope* ...

This is because not only is there the certainty that the world's darkness, and the influence of evil, *must* come to an end, but the realisation that present joys are only a foretaste of life in My near presence.

**No one will take away your joy.**

(John 16.22)

**A**s you come to experience My love, you begin to realise the mystery of existence, and desire to search no further!

You realise the truths inherent in the purpose of creation …

    darkness allowed;

    darkness overcome.

**Light has come into the world.**

(John 3.19)

The human experience of My love mirrors the great design of creation ...

Love as the first cause ...

Love surrendering itself to the consequences of a material creation ...

Love summing up all things as it triumphs over everything that is of darkness.

**God's eternal purpose accomplished in Christ Jesus our Lord.**

(Ephesians 3.11)

**M**y child, you are tempted to anticipate, fretfully, life's sterner demands. Remember My promise to go before you, so that you will be wonderfully strengthened, or will find that so many things will be *removed* from you.

Whatever trials you contemplate, tell Me of your thankfulness for the *outcome* ...

### The Lord will provide.

(Genesis 22.14)

Under no circumstances let hope die, because, as My chosen, it is yours *by right*.

You realise that hope, in its truest sense, cannot be found outside My love.

Hope ... because, knowing all your needs, I *will* bring everything right for you.

**I am your shield, your great reward.**

(Genesis 15.1)

**E**very present experience must be seen against the background of that to which this world moves – My triumph, and the vanquishing of evil for all time.

**It is My Father's good pleasure
to give you the Kingdom.**

(Luke 12.32)

**W**hen you are released from many of your worldly struggles, it will be a *permanent* release. Simply because you will have become a new person!

---

**He who began a good work in you
will carry it to completion.**

(Philippians 1.6)

There is always a way out of the prison of circumstances if you turn the focus of your attention to the One who loves you and guards you, the One who is grateful for *every* time that you come before Me. Fear of the future is taken away as you adjust your sights in this way.

**The crown of glory that will never fade.**

(1 Peter 5.4)

**M**y love's *covering* for every future aspect of your life.

Always looking beyond present circumstances to what that love is *pledged* to bring about.

### To be with the Lord for ever.

(1 Thessalonians 4.17)

Contemplating My love, the very darkest situation finds an opening for hope. The hope is based on the permanency of Myself compared with earth's trials. There, in your future, kept secure with My love, all pain at present experienced will be shed. This is no false hope ... it simply rests upon My unchanging nature. Let a little of that future security now comfort you, helping you to bear what otherwise you could not.

**Be of good courage;
I have overcome the world.**

(John 16.33)

The road to eternal life *begins* with love, and then leads to love, in all its fullness, at life's end.

**Come you blessed of My Father.**

(Matthew 25.34)

**W**here the manifestations of darkness in this world increase, do not despair, because I have promised that these things will herald My conquest. *All* manifestations of evil will be brought into subjection to Me.

Whisper your thanks to Me for victories to come – both in your own life and in the whole of creation.

**Whoever overcomes
will inherit all things.**

(Revelation 21.7)

My child, I want you to know that all things will be summed up in Me.

The power of darkness will be utterly destroyed, but not before it has wrought its final devastation.

Hearts will indeed fail them for fear, when they experience the conflict which will usher in My reign of peace.

When these things happen, many hearts will turn to Me ... but the urgent need is the *prepared* heart now.

I will come for the hearts which are ready; I will come for those who are earnestly looking for Me. I will come for those whose hearts are pure, because all that is of evil will be unable to stand in My presence.

**Watch and pray.**

(Matthew 26.41)

**M**y child, the days are short. Your mind, therefore, must be filled with Myself. You must cast out all that is unworthy, or which you know is not of lasting importance.

Be conscious of Me, all the time, as Light of the World.

Be found ready by feeding upon My word, and by your constant *submission* to Me.

### Blessed are all who wait for Him!

(Isaiah 30.18)

**M**y child, My look of love to embrace *all* ...

This is the love which carries you (with a lessening conscious effort) through life's complexities ... the complexities fading in their clamour for attention.

A journey in love, towards a destination of total love.

**Underneath are the everlasting arms.**

(Deuteronomy 33.27)

**W**hat you give to Me (in even fragmentary devotion and in wavering trust) is always repaid many times over, out of the bounty of My love.

I take each expression of gratitude, or of trust, and invest it with eternal value on your behalf.

In treading My road, you become increasingly lost in amazement at My attention to detail, and increasingly unable to express your gratitude adequately!

The expression of wonder about My care and provision becomes more and more heartfelt.

### ... things too wonderful for me.

(Psalm 131.1)

**R**emember that for those who trust Me as their shield, the destructive forces of the last days will *not* be able to prevail ...

My child, thank Me that as you remain steadfast for Me, I will indeed gather you into My arms ... where you will enjoy eternal *security*, in a new heaven and a new earth.

**The Lamb will be their Shepherd and lead them to springs of living water.**

(Revelation 7.17)

**M**y child, for the rest of your life ensure, above all, two things:

To see My love as the *answer* to every possible personal need or situation.

The cultivation of sheer trust in Me.

These things may sound, to some, an over-simplification, but they are the very essence of what is involved in living with Me.

Answers to your prayers *must* come if these two principles are observed; they are the true 'ingredients' of the eternal life which is *already* granted to you; they will *carry you forward* to the brightness of My immediate presence.

### Well done, good and faithful servant.

(Matthew 25.21)

# Specific Needs Index

Typical of the high praise for *I Am With You* received from Church leaders and from countless readers throughout the Christian denominations are these:

'*I Am With You* will bring peace and consolation to all who read it.'
> – *Cardinal Murphy-O'Connor*
> *Archbishop of Westminster*

'A very special book, which will bless countless people.'
> – *Prebendary John Pearce*
> *in the* Church of England Newspaper

'A lovely book of devotions. We use it daily.'
> – *Dr Donald English*
> *former President, Methodist Conference*

'I have never experienced such a closeness to Jesus.'
> – *Fran Gunning, USA*

'Reading *I Am With You* is a real joy.'
> – *Bishop John Crowley*

'A book which will deeply touch many people.'
> – *Fr Robert de Grandis, USA*

'The book has changed my life.'
> – *Fr Bernard SJ, India*

*Further copies of* Abide In My Love *and both Original Standard and Young People's editions of* I Am With You *are available from the Publisher:*

John Hunt Publishing
46a West Street, New Alresford
Hants, SO24 9AU, England

www.johnhunt-publishing.com

*or from:*

New Life
60 Wickstead Avenue, Luton
Beds. LU4 9DP, England

E-mail: books@new-life.demon.co.uk
http://www.new-life.co.uk

Bridge Books and Music
14 North Bridge Street, Sunderland
Tyne and Wear, SR5 1AB, England

# THE "I AM WITH YOU" FELLOWSHIP

Readers of Fr John`s inspired words may join the *I Am With You Fellowship*. All in the Fellowship are remembered in prayer and are encouraged to write about any particular need. To join, please send your name, address (incl.postcode), phone number and email address (if available) to I Am With You Foundation c/o Goodnews Books, 15 Barking Close, Luton Beds. LU4 9HG, UK. Please note that we also distribute mini copies of our books, free of charge, all over the world.

For further information, please contact us and visit our comprehensive website:

I Am With You Foundation
2 Lauradale Road
London N2 9LU, UK
Tel 020 8883 2665
www.iamwithyou.co.uk
email contact@iamwithyou.co.uk